God Don't Make Mistakes, People Do

People Do

Learning to Trust God in Difficult Times

God Don't Make Mistakes, People Do: Learning to Trust God in Difficult Times

Steven Carson

Published by Greater Works Publishing
A Division of Greater Works Enterprises, LLC
www.jpministries.org
2016

First Printing: 2016

ISBN 978-0-9975643-1-0

Greater Works Publishing
A Division of Greater Works Enterprises, LLC
Website:www.jpministries.org

Dedication

First I would like to thank God for giving me life and for giving us Jesus to die for our sins. I also thank Him for sending us the Holy Spirit to comfort and guide us through every step we take.

A special thanks to God for my beautiful, spontaneous, and supportive wife Lucrisha, along with my family and spiritual parents George W. and Dr. Jacqueline Stewart.

I Love you guys

Table of Contents

Introduction

I believe that it was not by mistake that you picked up this book! Hence the title of "God Don't Make Mistakes People DO!" Not only to just think about the title, but to think and look back over your life and notice that God does not make any mistakes. This book is about a personal relationship with God. Unlike most religious books you've read that were written by Pastors with theological degrees, this book is written by a common minister. This book is about different scenarios and situations that I've learned by reading the bible and what I experienced first-hand in my relationship with knowing Christ from a babe to maturing in Him.

To give you a brief history about myself I grew up in government housing in Tuscaloosa Alabama with my mother and three brothers after my parents divorced in 1985. While growing up I can remember getting baptized at age six and at that age there was an inkling that there was something out there that was bigger than what this world was presenting. I can remember being in Sunday school singing "Jesus loves the little children over the hills and everywhere" wondering, who is this Jesus who loves me? When I was 13, mother let my older brother talk her into letting us get baptized in the Church of Jesus Christ of Latter Day Saints. You may be asking yourself: 'How did this happen? Well, we were going to the boys and girls club and this young college student that would come to pick us up for mentoring was a Mormon who had a great influence over our lives at age thirteen and fourteen named Judy. She would try to get us to play tennis and run marathons etc. I guess she saw more in us than we did ourselves. I know you're thinking now how or why am I telling you all this? Well, it will all come out in the wash. You know the wash the bible says in Eph. 5:26 that he might sanctify her, having cleansed her by the washing of water with the word. That "her" it speaks of in this text is the church and this is all part of how all things work together for the good of those who love the Lord and are called according to his purpose. So in short terms, keep reading, I pray it will all come together by the time you finish reading this book. Continuing on… With Questions??? While taking our second dip of deliverance our grandfather was a devoted deacon to this holiness church where the Pastor of the church would lay hands on the people.

There, most of the women would speak in this language that I had no idea what they were saying and my mama would put us in the line to get prayed for. Standing in those lines I could always remember thinking "what in the world is this man going to do to us, what is going to happen when those hands the preacher had drenched in olive oil touched us, and what did the oil mean?" He'd get us up there and scream at us while he put his oily hand on our heads and it would make us feel like he was pushing us back. But we were determined not to fall because we didn't understand why all the other people were falling down! What was the oil for and why was he putting his oily hand on our heads? So, we would always walk away with oily foreheads and even then I had questions that were never answered. One, because I didn't know who to ask and two I didn't know how to present any of the questions I was thinking. (Do you know what I'm talking about?) Being in a place where you want to know more about God and His being.

Running everywhere trying to touch a God who's had His hand on us the whole time wondering, God where are you? Who are you? Also can we meet one day? Little did I know He would one day reveal all these questions later on in my life and I believe He will reveal them to you as well. I'd go on to date a girl in high school who went to this Seventh Day Sanctified filled church where there was a woman Pastor who would preach like the walls were coming down. My girlfriend's mom was okay with us dating as long as I went to church with them. While going with them their Pastor said one day that she was "intimate with Jesus". Now, I didn't see her husband and I didn't know if his name was Jesus, but it was yet another experience I just didn't understand.

One day something else interesting happened, well three things happened that I will tell you about that all had questions tied to them. The first was the entire church was praising God with music, amen's and shouting. Then this one lady started speaking in a language that made everybody in the church STOP what they were doing and they ALL listened to her. After she got through talking another lady would get up and say "this is what the Spirit of the Lord Says". Wow, finally some explanation, but really I was still confused! What just happen? The second was that my girlfriend's little brother who was six years old, was playing like he was talking as one of those ladies in the church, being playful, got what I now know was "caught by the Spirit", he was six and couldn't stop talking in tongues and crying trying to stop! I thought this was spooky and exciting at the same time, that a God who I could not see would take a child, who made the mistake of mocking God, get touched by His Spirit. What would happen if I play with God? Third was when my girlfriend and her family left the church because one day they found out that the Pastor was doing bad things and threatening her church followers saying; that if they left the church they would die once they left! Will they die and who was being disobedient in that church? Sometime later my mother had complications with fluid around her heart and after a doctor, that evidently made a mistake, put a pace maker in her heart and one of the wires came loose in the pacemaker and my mother died! Now, my mother did not go to that Seventh Day Adventist Church, but she was a praying woman! I would watch my mom as I was growing up and I'd noticed she would occasionally just sit and stare out the window.

As she would sit lost in her gazes, I just knew she was reflecting on life. Yes, she made mistakes, but she was a great woman and not just because she was my mother. She was a great woman because, even though she was divorced, she raised four men on her own and was able to keep a smile on her face through all of the hell she experienced in life. She also had a giving spirit that made her great. When she cooked, she would make enough for our friends and family in the project to come by and get a plate. My mother could sing like an angel, but I guess it was time for her to sing with God, because he called her home at the age of 40. I remember the week that she passed because interesting events occurred on the day she died. That week my brother who was one year older than me and my twin was visiting my mother in the hospital where she'd gone into cardiac arrest. While the same night before that happened I was on the phone with her and I could remember falling asleep in her bed. As I slept I had a dream that my mother was going down into a grave with these rose pedals that were pink and blue falling with her as she was going down. I woke up with anxiety and tears falling from my face like a river and for the first time I prayed a sincere prayer.

That prayer was "God, please let my mama come home Please let my Mama Come HOME!!!" That prayer was soon answered the same week on Friday, she came home and we hugged her and enjoyed her that night and we didn't want to go to sleep because we were all so happy that night. She said that night "that this year was going to be her year" in joyfulness. That next morning it was 3:06am on the alarm clock as I woke up on my arm that went numb laying sideways it seemed as if my hand was waving goodbye to me. I knew it was her, in my sleepy mind because every time my fingers would bend down I could feel fingertips on the palm of my hand and it was not that normal tingling feeling your hand gets when the blood tries to come back I your veins. Although I was sleepy I remember saying "bye Mama" as if I knew she was leaving. That morning when I got up I heard a cry that I never heard before from my brother who laid next to her to make sure she would be ok. He found her body first as my twin and I walked into the bedroom where we tried to stop our brother who was trying to wake her up because we knew she was not coming back. I thought then that my life had just changed. All of this occurred during my senior year in high school; we not only had to face what was next but we also had to realize that our world just CHANGED. I went on to college after graduating from C-High commuting from Tuscaloosa to Birmingham AL determined to try to make something of myself. Although there were a lot of challenges in that same year I would have to share them throughout this book so I'll fast forward just a bit. I went on to graduate from college the first time and attended a university to try to earn another degree, but ended up pledging a fraternity, collecting mistakes, and a marriage at age 23 where I would end up divorced by the time I was 26. With two children a step-son and at a crossroad thinking my life had changed again. After my divorce I could only think what did I do wrong over the years? What mistakes did I make that would have me in this position feeling that I had no purpose in life! It was then that I knew I had to get closer to a God that I've prayed to my whole life, but now it was really time to get to know Him. I didn't go right to Him after the divorce it took three more years of bad choices before I finally fell on my face and gave it all to God. I walked away from the job not knowing what to do or where to go. I went from making a 40-thousand-dollar base salary, not including overtime, to not knowing where my next meal would come from. Did I just make a mistake? Or did I just make the greatest move I ever made in my Life? I spent a year in a half living in vehicles and crashing wherever God had led me. God doesn't make mistakes people do, but will this mistake grow me up in a way I never known? Or could this have been the best paid seminary or Bible College a man could buy from what I've learned to call my wilderness? You will see in this book not just the mistakes I've made, but of situations I saw in my wilderness of others that God had mended and made for a greater cause of understanding. I pray it blesses you.

Chapter 1 – The Process (King David and I)

This entire book is about the process because once you've acknowledged that Jesus is God's only begotten son you must first understand that you are saved, but then there's the process. A main principle in understanding the process is knowing that God is purging you for your purpose. Your purpose has to be pure and holy or else God can't use you for His Glory. Also you must understand that God's plan must go on because God said so and if God cannot use you, he can use someone else. This does not mean that you will not enter Heaven, but it does mean that you cannot be used for the task in that season.

King David

In 1 Samuel chapter 16 around verse 13 David is anointed as to be the next King of Israel and at that moment he was saved. The bible calls David a man after God's on heart (in 1 Samuel 13:14) three chapters before he was even anointed but he too had a process. He served as a shepherd, he killed the lion and the bear and while serving he killed Goliath with a stone. These things were just the beginning of the process because even after the people saw how blessed David was he remained humble until God's appointed time. He dealt with jealousy – the time the people realized the power of David they exalted him greater than King Saul in his position. This was a big problem with Saul so much that it was driving him insane knowing that it was something so special about his servant that he just knew David deserved his position more than himself. While Saul was jealous, David still served by playing a harp for the very person who was jealous of him not in spite of Saul but with a servant's heart (1 Samuel 19:9) David walked in forgiveness. Chapters go on to show Saul waging war on David, but during David's process he would not buck against God's anointed people.

David's Mistake

Then there is the Big mistake of David, he decided not to go out to the battle field one day and was enticed when he saw a woman bathing outside his courts and asked for her to come to his quarters. Her name was Bathsheba and she was Uriah's wife – David had sex with another man's wife and got her pregnant. All of this occurred after all that God had done for David by answering all of his prayers and showing him the way out of trouble. Now David would open a can of worms that he would regret down the road. David's mistake claimed the life of Bathsheba's husband as well as the life of the child conceived in adultery. David would later regain favor with God toward the end of his lifetime and had the desire to build a temple for God, but God would not let him build the temple, instead God said He would build it for David's family. (2 Samuel 7) David couldn't build the temple due to blood on his hands, but God's promise would still remain with the house of David forever. Why the story of David? Because I can see so many examples of so many people including myself who want to serve God, but through the process we too often make mistakes! In the last part of David's story, we see that even though God would not let him build the temple, he was going to allow his son to build it. In the midst of this promise, God also said that He would be a father to David's son and chasten him as needed. WOW! There is so much meat in that alone; that God would be a father to David's son and maintain favor with him and chasten him because of his love for David. The honor in getting God's attention like this we could only imagine to have such an honor but… we do! *Once we've accepted Jesus as our Lord and savior we have become David's seed by being adopted into the Kingdom through Christ Jesus.

Then there was ME!

I once had a friend while in the "Geneses" part of my process; he would say that David was his favorite man of the Bible. I didn't understand it at first, but I do now. Around the age fourteen I just knew that there was something I had to do for God and I didn't quite understand it until the appointed time. I would pray bolder prayers then than I do now because I was humble and as a child just wanting to do the right thing I could remember praying this prayer: "God whatever you want me to do please let me do whatever I want to do until it's time, let me be with every woman I want to be with and let me make good money too! Like a white man around $15 an hour. Amen"

So clearly I remember that prayer and yes I was a horny fourteen-year-old boy with the wrong motive in mind. Yet! I still prayed a prayer to my Father without worry of every wrong word that may come out of my mouth. Isn't this how Jesus said we must come to him like a little child though? I was a child with only the understanding that "God I know you are out there and I hope and pray you are listening!" But just as David was anointed as a shepherd boy I got my first promise from God then. How do I know ("Selah" which means: to pause and reflect on these words!) I could now in my life pause and reflect that even back then God answered my prayers! God would answer my prayers later on as I went through school earning certifications and an Associates' Degree in Electronic Engineering at a tech school in 99. Also to catch you up to this story I started working in a tier one car supplier company in Birmingham AL that started me out making $14.50 an hour. I started working at that job with guys my age with similar backgrounds as I had. So, let me pause to tell you that if God has presented you with an offer just short of what you've prayed for, just take time out to shout because He is getting ready to "DO" something greater! After a year I got promoted to a job in my field of study at that plant that started me out at $16 an hour and I was the second minority to work in the department ever at the job. Now won't God do it?

As a child I prayed for a job that would make me $15 an hour and God would one up me, by giving me another dollar over what I prayed for. If you noticed I also mentioned I was the second minority in the department that meant that the rest of the guys were white males and we had nineteen guys in the department. God just gave me a job like a white man, just like that horny naïve fourteen-year-old boy had prayed for. God is able to do exceedingly abundantly over all I can ask think or imagine Eph. 3:20. All this for little old me and I had not begun to know God for myself yet! What I've yet to tell you is that at this time of promise and prosperity I was married to my first wife with a newborn baby, a step-son and a daughter I had out of wed-lock by another woman. I was being blessed by a God who looked past my sins and heard and answered my prayers I assumed, because I at least wanted to change from the place where I started my family. I wanted to have more for my children because growing up in the projects I knew that it wasn't the place I wanted them to grow up in. I had this thing that I could see already in my head how my children were going to be and I knew the right ingredients to make it all happen, but first things first I had to get myself in order. My first wife and I were not always on the same page most of what we've done was trying to move forward with each other not knowing where to go. God was not the center of our marriage and like King David unfaithfulness tore our house whole apart. I got enticed with unfaithfulness and adultery just as King David. After being blessed with what I know God answered and working the job I know God gave me, out of disobedience I lost the opportunity of seeing first-hand how I saw the children growing up to be!

This showed me a lot of God not making a mistake; we did, by not letting Him be the center of our life, but rather a hope in our road. I say hope in our road because if you don't first plan you plan to fail and by moving forward on our journey not knowing where to go we made the first mistake in not planning. Habakkuk 2:2 KJV in the b) clause of the verse says to "Write the vision, and make it plain upon tables." Not knowing who Habakkuk was, if you had asked us at the time who it was, we would have thought it was someone we went to school with. So much dysfunction was going on in my life. You see, we were like most believers who think they are doers in Christ, we were just hoping for change, and trying to grow in wealth with our own process without God. He has to be the center of it all; I now know but then, I was toh-up to the flo-up. We were divorced in 2006 and I spun out of control with mistakes, mishaps and misunderstandings. I would start by putting my troubles in bottles and trying to satisfy my emotions in women, but I maintained my job at the plant just staying afloat in our economy. After playing pin the tail on the donkey for so long with my life I found myself being in insanity doing the same thing over and over again looking for different results an being the donkey I found where the pin went also by sticking it to myself. I got so tired of me I had to give it God. One night I lay prostrate on the floor of my apartment and said God I give up. It was that next day I began church hopping trying to find a church home, I needed to find a church where I could belong.

Trying to find a Church Home

I realized that I'd never belonged to a church as a real member before; I would attend and go when my mother would take us growing up, but never taking a class and saying this is it! There was this church close to the apartment I thought it would be good to join because it was so close to the job that I thought it could be it. Well, I visited the church a couple of weeks trying to see if it would be a place I could grow. I stood up, to joined their church one day and started taking the classes until one day this deacon approached me with the wrong attitude that made me want to leave. I only had one class left to being a full-fledge member when a deacon came to me and said "hey guy what's your name?" I told him my name, knowing he already knew it, he then says to me "I probably didn't know it because I haven't seen you in a while." I had only missed the previous Sunday of class because I went to see my children. Life for me was critical because I seriously wanted to know God and my life was in shambles; while sarcasm was not the way I was looking for salvation. So I left and went back to my old ways drinking and partying trying to fill a void of comfort because thus far in my eyes the church had no answers for me. Until one day after partying I was lying in the bed one Sunday wanting to go to church. I woke up with the radio on next to the lamp on the nightstand from it was a voice saying: "Are you growing where you Going?" I thought to myself "no!" to answer the question sense I was just getting started in a church and I've already relapsed to darkness so, I needed to be at that church so I can grow! That day I got up with a friend and went to church. I sat in the balcony listening to the preacher and it seemed as if he had been drinking my kool-aid and up in my business because it seemed as if he was talking directly to me! It was the same voice I had heard on the radio and at the end of that service I went down to the altar and joined the church. This time it was like never before; I could remember crying like a baby not knowing why, but it felt like I just found home. Two weeks later I helped pump gas at a gas giveaway the church held and it was amazing to see people being blessed by a church that gave rather than getting the people to give. So, I went through my classes started serving within the first month just wanting to help. I found myself going to the biggest church I have ever attended, but the most connected I ever felt to a church.

Just Getting Started

Even though I found a church home and things seemed as if they were headed in into the right direction, little did I know that this was just the beginning of my part of my process! You see getting saved (confessing that Jesus died and rose from the dead) and finding a place to grow is just the starting line of the race that's not giving to the strong, but to him that endures to the end. I only just found a place to be taught and mentored. Then I would find myself reading the bible and wanting to read it. Yes, there is a difference in reading and wanting to read because when you are just reading the bible you miss out on so many details that matter, but wanting to read the bible you develop a hunger that would have your face in the book not wanting to come up to for air to breathe. Like a child wanting to get to know what their parents were like I started asking questions I knew only God could answer. I made a statement to God in prayer saying "God I want you more than I want food." This thought came from when I saw a movie where Jesus fed the five thousand and people wanted to follow him after they saw the miracle. Jesus turned to the flock of people and said "do not work for food that spoils, but for food that endues to eternal life." I wanted God more than I wanted food so I was lead to a reading plan that would have me to read the bible in this pattern:

- For Breakfast- Genesis all of Chapter one in the KJV Bible (King James Version)
- For Lunch- Genesis all of Chapter one in the MSG Bible (Message)
- For Dinner- Genesis all of Chapter one in the NIV Bible (New International Version)

*I would read in this pattern, but I would finish my reading before I ate all the meals!

This went on for me every day until the middle part of Leviticus and what this was doing for me was transforming my mind. I could remember even from growing up people would quote scripture and go to a verse off the top of their heads and I would think that it was all impossible, but I now find myself doing the same thing. I was reading and find myself sharing the word of God to people at work and also trying to visit fellow employees at their church. I was not afraid to share the word of God with anybody. I fellowshipped with many people at work, because work took up most of my time and since that's where I was; that's where I shared the word of God! Let me pause and say that often times where God wakes you up is where He wants you to start talking and crawling for Him. I found out that God used a Donkey to talk in the bible in Numbers 22:28 to speak to Balaam for beating him when Balaam was about to make a mistake to go the wrong way! I thought isn't that interesting that God would use what we call a jackass to speak to the one acting like one just to give him a warning.

These were the things I was learning from random people God was sending my way and I was learning the word of God for myself. I made time to share, but work, and bills and stress were still in my everyday environment. I had a boss who really did not like me. He liked my work but he didn't like me fellowshipping with people at work. He told me one day that he wanted to write me up in his office for my work ethic talking to people on the floor. Although that day he didn't write me up it was a sure sign that I was being watched. Not only was he watching me he would pile on the work load and assign me mandatory weekends to work. When I would put in notice to take off to visit my children; he would make me stay and work. It was pretty rough because I was making good money and even though I wanted those days off I really did need the money; I just really wanted to see my children. My money was stretched due to bills, child support, and loans – I really needed to get things in order. You see even though I wanted a break I believe God pushed my boss to keep me in the fire. We as people in this day and time don't fight like they did in the old days, not as much as physical fighting but mentally fighting. Fighting not just for what was right but to make things right doing whatever it takes to put things in order.

Before we go on lets quickly review the mistakes and see how God is starting to work some things for my good and I pray it's giving you glimpse of your journey. My first mistake really started as a child wanting to do what the world had to offer before letting God take control of my life. God honored my prayer later on, but I've managed to learn bad habits leading up to my place of purpose. My second mistake was using the habits I learned and taking them into marriage while not being equipped for marriage (I call this trying to do a good thing, but not doing a God thing). This mistake ended with me getting a divorce and a lifestyle full of turmoil. While I was making the mistakes God was planning my future; He knew that I would get those promises because he's God and he also knew I would screw them up. Also like King David who had to serve under a man who did not like him I had to serve and respect a boss who didn't like me, but what God also knew is that I would do anything to try to get it all back together even if it took losing everything! Why? Because I was just that hard headed and God doesn't make any mistakes I did.

Chapter 2 – The Hearing Test (Samuel and I)

The boy Samuel was serving GOD under Eli's direction. This was at a time when the revelation of GOD was rarely heard or seen. One night Eli was sound asleep (his eyesight was very bad—he could hardly see). It was well before dawn; the sanctuary lamp was still burning. Samuel was still in bed in the Temple of GOD, where the Chest of God rested. Then GOD called out, "Samuel, Samuel!" Samuel answered, "Yes? I'm here." Then he ran to Eli saying, "I heard you call. Here I am." Eli said, "I didn't call you. Go back to bed." And so he did. GOD called again, "Samuel, Samuel!" Samuel got up and went to Eli, "I heard you call. Here I am." Again Eli said, "Son, I didn't call you. Go back to bed." (This all happened before Samuel knew GOD for himself. It was before the revelation of GOD had been given to him personally.) GOD called again, "Samuel!"—the third time! Yet again Samuel got up and went to Eli, "Yes? I heard you call me. Here I am." That's when it dawned on Eli that GOD was calling the boy. So Eli directed Samuel, "Go back and lie down. If the voice calls again, say, 'Speak, GOD. I'm your servant, ready to listen.'" Samuel returned to his bed. Then GOD came and stood before him exactly as before, calling out, "Samuel! Samuel!" Samuel answered, "Speak. I'm your servant, ready to listen." GOD said to Samuel, "Listen carefully."

1 Samuel 3:1-11 (MSG)

Have you ever had a hearing test done before? If not, let me explain the process. When having a hearing test done you would have to sit in this box with a pair of headphones and a push button hanging inside of it. The test person would then ask you to put the headphones on your head. Then he would tell you that you are going to hear a series of "beep's" and whenever you hear the beep push the button that's in your hand. These beeps would get loud then get very quiet and they would go from one ear to the next beep... beep... beep! So since I've told you that I worked in the car manufacturing environment we had to be tested in order to work in the building because of all the noise that was in the plant. Therefore, you would have to pass "the hearing test" or otherwise you couldn't work in the building. Just as a person could not work in our building, the same applies to the Kingdom of Heaven. How else can you do work for God unless you can hear from the Holy Spirit? More importantly, how can you do work for God unless you accept Jesus as your Lord and personal savior? The answers to the questions are these: you cannot do it without these tools. If you haven't accepted Jesus as your Lord and personal savior, please say this prayer with me:

> "Lord Jesus I repent of my sins, please come into my life, I believe that you died on the cross for my sake and my sins. I believe that you also rose on the third day and you are seated at the right-hand of the father, In Jesus Christ name we pray." Amen

On behalf of the Lord and Savior; I would like to thank you and welcome you to a life that is new, forgetting your past. Now to the hearing test, did you know that as we read how Samuel was called by God not one, two, three, but four times before he responded! He made the mistake of not responding to God, but ran to man for an answer of what he was hearing. Isn't that just the way we respond to God so often when we hear we know is God and we run to a man to get their opinion first? Good thing in the passage was that Samuel ran to his mentor, someone he knew had his best interests at heart. We, on the other hand, take advice from too many people who just want conversation. Eli,

Samuel's mentor took him in years ago when his mother gave him up to God. Eli spent a lot of his time in Gods temple, a God fearing man and even he didn't hear God calling Samuel. Even though he knew God for himself and evidently could not have been too far from Samuel for him to ask him what he'd said. We see that God was checking Samuel's hearing then once he responded to God, God gave him instructions. One thing as believers in our day and time living under grace is this; when God speaks it's not a suggestion, it's an order!

Now that we are living under grace through Jesus Christ, some of us believe that we can always get away with sin with the famous phrase "God knows my Heart." The truth of the matter is he does know your heart, but we tend to be mistaken forgetting the fact that God put everything in us and knows all. What God wants us to do with our heart, our will and our ways is to line up with his will. I did not understand this principle myself on so many occasions when I was getting to know Jesus for myself.

Then there was Me!

I remember riding to work very early in the morning listening to a gospel CD. I'd been listening to for weeks trying to train my ears to hear gospel music opposed to the rap and r&b ears I've had for so long. Between the seventh and eighth track I heard a voice give me instruction and I knew I was not talking to myself. What it told me was this, "When you get to work find Jim and when you find him tell him that he is doing a good job and don't stop doing what you are doing." Even though I didn't understand how I heard that at the time I had a good idea that it was from the Lord. I said alone in that ride out loud "ok God if that's what you want me to do then that's what I'll do." I remember parking and walking into the plant, going into the locker room to put on my work boots, I straightened my uniform and walked on the floor. Now, the plant was very big about two football fields long and one football field wide. When I walked out on the floor I saw someone coming out of the bathroom, oddly the only one coming towards me from the wide end of the plant, it was Jim. Now Jim was this older guy around 57 years old and a preacher who wore these glasses with his hat tight on his head snuggled close to his glasses that'd stood about 5 foot 8 inches tall. I had no idea what was going on in his life nor did I understand why I was to tell Jim anything pertaining to his life.

I caught up with him and told him saying; "Jim I don't know why I'm telling you this, but something told me to tell you that you are doing a good job and don't stop doing what you're doing." Not knowing what that meant to him he stood there and looked up at me dead in my eyes then slightly tilted his head to the left and tears began to flow down his face! He said to me; "I don't know what God is doing to you but…" that was all he could say. Thinking to myself wow, how could a simple word affect his life in that instance and why would God use me to say it! Now that I think about it I can see that God was testing my hearing to see if I'd listen and respond to the call. Thinking back also, on how many "times" I heard the call and not respond or how many blessings have "I" held back from people because I hung up on the call.

There was this one incident in college when I attended this church where the pastor asked if I would be his youth pastor. At that time all I could think about was the fact that I didn't want to mess with no one's life and cause them to slip because I had flaws myself. So, I turned it down not knowing then that I was making the mistake in delaying my destiny from the opportunity to learn ministry. Often times we could turn down an opportunity from God because we see the mess we've created or standing in. We look at what we think about ourselves instead of seeing what it is God sees about us, but now I've come to find out that God can take a mess of things and make it beautiful. He will give you beauty for ashes and He will take the foolish of things to confound the wise. God also plays in dirt too I'll tell you how I know, because He, in the beginning, took dirt to make man in the first place. God doesn't make mistakes people do, so if God is pushing you into something "Trust" that He has his own reasons.

After speaking to Jim, days went on and I heard another instruction that said get ready to leave your job and I will let you know when. I simply said "ok God" while thinking; I am almost topped out in pay and I'm on days a position I've been praying about for years and now I'm saying "ok" but my spirit was calm in saying ok because I trusted him. With this on my mind all that week to Sunday I was walking to church because my truck didn't have that much gas and it wasn't a long walk at all carrying only my bible and 20 dollars in my pocket. Walking, the simple word ringing in my ear was just trust him, just trust him and just trust him. I arrived at the church that morning assigned to the security ministry post. I stood to the far right from the stage of the theater we were in because church was held in a school at the time. Doing my job in ministry manning my post and listening to the word from the pulpit, I contemplated in my head what God was saying about my job. I also contemplated on whether to trust God with my money because all I had was twenty dollars and my paycheck was already spent. How was I going to trust God with all of these different thoughts? Well, in that same service, when the pastor finished, the assistant pastor stood up as if he heard everything God spoke to me. He stepped up and said "it's time to give unto God, Don't You Trust Him?" Now this might be common to you, but for me I'd knew that I kept hearing "just trust him" on the walk all the way to church. So I said "ok God" and took all that I had in my pocket and put it in the offering bucket. I felt relieved that I gave it all up and didn't know what to think from it, but it felt good knowing I just obeyed God to the fullest.

Keep in mind that I just walked to church because I didn't have gas to get to church so, how was I going to get to work! I walked out of that school that day making sure the pastor left safely and the co-pastor left safely. Though honestly I really didn't want to walk back home after standing up the whole service and I thought someone was going to ask if I'd needed a ride, but no one did. I then asked God: "I trusted you, I heard you, and walked to church just to walk back? Hmph! I felt sad but this was a start of me growing out of immaturity. You see, often times we want God to give us simple things that we can get for ourselves, but God wants you to try your faith, He pushes towards things and accomplishments you cannot see yourself grabbing hold of so that He can see himself manifest in you. I walked home and when I got there with the thought "well God I don't know how I'm going to get to work this week, but I trust you. I laid down and slept well for about four hours and something woke me up and told me to call a friend that I knew would sometimes be in my area. So I called and said hey are you going to be around my area Monday I need a ride? The response to me was no I won't, but have you called "Dee"? Now Dee and I had been friends for five years but we had a falling out because of our egos, for a lack of better words I responded to him no I haven't, not explaining why, and I got off the phone still thinking "God I trust you."

I laid down again then my phone rang and the voice I hear on the other line was "Dee", "was up bro you need a ride to work, maybe we can work something out because I got to be out of town for a few days while I get my car worked on!" I had to pause for a second to think about what God just did in this instance. Dee called me without any hesitation and with no grudge in him at all towards me. He even had the audacity to want to help! Wow, after all this time I was the only one holding the grudge and breaking the friendship that we'd built as brothers, it wasn't him it was me and God used my situation to mend a friendship. I was not only trusting God but he also was testing my hearing to see if I would hear Him and trust His instruction. Keeping up with the reading of the word while going to work, my routine didn't stop until one day I was cleaning up my toolbox and a work buddy came up to me and asked "Hey man are you leaving us?" Before I could respond to him a voice told me to tell him yes I am leaving. He was in shock because he was just kidding around, but God was preparing me for my next move in my life for Him. I came in the next day and put in my two-week notice! Again I was feeling relieved because I was obeying the command of God and I was so willing to see where this was going to take me; after seeing what God did the last time I trusted Him I was ready to go. Two weeks of saying farewells, goodbyes, and with my heart beating fast on the last day I heard an instruction from God and it was critical it said; "Don't ask no man for nothing and Don't listen to no man, but Me!" Now if I didn't trust God I would have thought I was getting hood winked because I was walking out of the door and this is what he was telling me! But I didn't resort to that kind of thinking, I trusted that it was God talking to me and I was all in! God doesn't make mistakes people do and I knew this time trusting Him was not a mistake. In fact, it was going to teach me to trust Him even more. Knowing I couldn't ask for nothing if I ran low on funds or food would be tight, but God said trust him and that's all I had left. Now, I did make the mistake of thinking that just because God took me from my job that He was getting ready to drop the bombshell of blessings over me like crazy, but I was highly mistaken. You see God was getting ready to take me into my wilderness, I didn't know it then but I know it now and I will tell you about it in chapter 3. You just have to stick around. He was just checking my hearing so He could lead me, guide me and order my steps. Also in chapter three you will see how God has done great things in leading me to the right people, doing miracles, constantly checking my hearing and growing me in ministry. Take a quick second and ask yourself, are you *Listening?*

Chapter 3 – Overcoming the Wilderness (Testimony)

And they have defeated him by the Blood of the Lamb and by their testimony. And they did not love their lives so much that they were afraid to die.

Revelation 12:11 (NLT)

And they have defeated him by the Blood of the Lamb and by their testimony. Who are we defeating you ask? The enemy of course, we all have one common enemy of the Kingdom of Heaven and that's Satan. From back then up until now the enemy has influenced our lives. Since the Garden of Eden we were born into sin through our flesh where he dominantly resided individually in our inner ME. We overcome him, defeat him, and are delivered from him by the renewing of our minds through Christ Jesus. In renewing our minds, we become slaves to Christ by obeying His word and His commands. It sounds serious, I know, but there is joy in knowing that Jesus will never leave you nor forsake you. When you trust that, you will know that obeying His will and His way is the best thing anyone can ever do! God doesn't make mistakes people do!

For me, my experience in learning to know about God the Father, God the Son, and God the Holy Spirit for myself is what taught me a lot when I left the job. With the instructions I heard given to me by the Spirit "don't ask no man for nothing and don't listen to no man, but Me." In my head I couldn't think, but I was getting ready to learn how to trust God! After hearing and obeying to leave my job I thought my assignment was to start my own business in creating platforms for people of purpose. So there was this church located close to my job that would allow me to get started. I would have people come up to share their purposes and it was a good turnout for the times I did do it. I knew there was something more out there. My cousin and his wife came to one of my events and he said that they enjoyed it and it reminded him of something one of his relatives on his dad's side of the family was doing. One day after picking my children up from out of town I came to Tuscaloosa to relax with my cousin and family just to be around family. Then my cousin's phone rings; after going out to answer it he returns saying that another family member in Birmingham needs our help and asked if I would come. Yes, sure I replied because the kids were safe with my aunt and the drive was less than an hour away.

We pull up and I had this study bible I carried around everywhere because that was a part of my reading assignment so I laid it on the dashboard that day of his car. His cousin met us as we were getting out of the car and says to us "that looks like a preacher's bible right there"; and walks to me and says "hey preacher." Now all I knew was that he knew my cousin and he didn't know me, but it was something very peculiar about him. He was a fifty-six-year-old man who stood about six feet tall and weighed one hundred and eighty-five pounds. I later found out that my cousin was calling him cousin, but he was actually my cousin's father's first cousin. Say that again three times fast, you can see why most readers look fast over the genealogy parts of the bible. So, we greeted respectfully and helped loading a Stage-play set into a trailer and then after that we prayed. I was thinking about how awesome it was to be going out on a limb for God and he would find us a place to pray for encouragement. I stood in the living room of his house and cried while I prayed just loving on God for His goodness and His mercy. I asked him if there was anything I could help him with to give me a call so we exchanged numbers and my cousin and I went back to Tuscaloosa.

He kept calling me as we formed a relationship and before I knew it he was mentoring me in ministry and he just went from being my cousin's dad's first cousin to my father in ministry. What a joy to know that God would not leave you nor forsake you, but also give you a mentor to cover you in your walk in ministry. You remember the story in chapter two of this book when God kept calling Samuel to see if he was listening; well Eli was Samuel's mentoring father at that time. Samuel's mother gave him up to God when he was born in 1 Sam. 1 after praying for him. Then she only came to visit her son "once" a year and that was just to bring him an ephod, something only the priest wore. She kept the faith in believing that God would bless her with a child and didn't waver when everyone around her was getting blessed as well. That's a note to you if you are believing that God will bless you with something; there is a blessing in patience that God will fulfill your prayers even while you are seeing everyone getting bless around you.

Before I moved out of place I served in the church I attended doing prison ministry, group ministry, security ministry and doing anything the church needed, I was devoted to the church. Every time the doors of the church were open I just knew it was something I had to do! So what I decided to do first with my last paycheck and the rest of my 401k was to go down south to be close to my children I've longed to be close to for three years. I stayed with a college buddy of mine while I was down and had the chance to be able to pick my kids up from school and take them to school for a while and it felt normal. Although, I really didn't know why or where God was leading me in in my journey I was at peace. I remember around this time I got a call from two high school friends of mine who I haven't heard from in a while – they said to me "what's up man how you been?" Before they could say anything else I said "I just got to let you guys know I'm living for Jesus now."

I quickly had to make my disclaimer because the guys were not bad guys, I just knew that I had to warn them before we would have gone into conversation that I wouldn't have found comfortable or healthy for what God was doing for me. This was a small victory for me because I remember at times someone would want to change the subject from Jesus and I would passively agree to terms with them and go along to get along. Thank God that I was learning how to change because through reading for myself I found that in scripture it says; "Whoever is ashamed of me and my words, the Son of Man will be ashamed of them when he comes in his glory and in the glory of the Father and of the holy angels." Wow, so many times I was being ashamed of my greatest asset and didn't know it. Down in the area where my children were living I found myself going back to the church where the pastor asked me to be his youth pastor. I had to go back to apologize for turning down the position and asked him if it was anything I could help him with. He responded that the church that they were in was going to be bought and that they had to go to another location; and if I could help him with that it would be helpful. So he took me over to see the new building and it was a very rough old building, a storefront in an old downtown district location. As we stood in the middle of the rubble that looked as if a tornado came in and destroyed just the inside of the place; the pastor says to me "if you could help me with this we would be happy to have you. I agreed to help and I realized that was my first assignment in ministry.

I could remember going through how they wanted things done and how I had the skill set to do the things they needed done. Most of the things that needed to be done I was able to do because I either learned about it in school or the knowledge came from skills I picked up over my life. They gave me keys to the church and I would be there praising God listening to gospel music while I worked, praying and meditating on what God was doing in my life. As I read through the Bible, I saw how God established the tabernacle and how it applied to me building a church for the people. You see, not that it's anything wrong with going to other countries to do mission, but even thou this is the Land of the Free and the Home of the Brave, these people need missions too. God is everywhere and at the same time he is "Omnipotent". So I know that this was my first mission to help rebuild the temple while God was rebuilding mine. We did this within the 30-day window the church had and that church is still there to this day. After the church was done, it was time for me to prepare to leave Troy.

Making the final round of picking my kids up from school I kept this necklace made out of yarn and cardboard paper in an image of a man scripted with Ecc. 3:1. The verse read "there is a time for everything, and a season for everything under the Heaven. I kept it hanging on the rear view mirror and after picking Khalil up from pre-K (my youngest son at the time). We drove to the middle school to pick-up his older brother. While waiting in line there was a heavy storm brewing outside the vehicle with hard rain. Then out of nowhere my son ask "daddy what is that?"

I turned to see what he was talking about and he was pointing to the necklace I had hanging on the rear view mirror. I told him that I'd got it from church and asked if he would like to see it? His innocent 4-year-old response was, no! Then he asks what is it doing outside? I replied it's raining. He then said to me that it was raining down here but, not raining up there. I figure he was talking about Heaven, so I ask are you talking about Heaven? He'd go on to say "yep daddy they are up playing basketball. Every time they dunk the ball they go through the clouds and come back up!"

First I thought, what an imagination! Then as I thought to put it together he never read the verse and I didn't read it to him. But, what I was getting out of this conversation is that God was talking to me through him. That no matter how bad things look down here on earth even in storms there will always be joy in Heaven. Also another way to look at it is that adults can easily make the mistake in looking at children's thoughts as cute idea's. For example, the boy in the story of feeding the five thousand people not including women and children! The child did not have a cute imagination as my son did but, Jesus had a great idea to use what the child had on his plate to feed a multitude of people. I remember crying and kissing my kids goodbye because the work I had in Troy was over, but while I will never be through with them, it was time to head back to Birmingham. Yet the instructions from God still remained to not ask no-man for nothing and to not listen to no man, but Me! So as time went on I studied and served where ever I saw the need to serve as I went to and fro. I remember my best friend seeing my walk in fasting and wanting to do something different as he would tell me at times when I wanted to go back to old ways of thinking. "Bro you can't quit you got too many people looking at you now they are looking up to what you're doing."

That was very comforting to know that he had my back even though he was familiar to the old me in the streets. You see your walk with Jesus and getting to know him for yourself is the most intimate relationship you can ever have because; unlike man, when you have a one on one communication with God he will allow you to have contact with Him through everyone and everything at the same time. This could be through helping people, people helping you or just God's undeserving favor upon our lives. That's also why we have to have an attentive ear to what the Holy Spirit is saying for us to do.

At the Same place at the Same time

There was a time I was just riding along meditating on what the spirit wanted me to do and then I heard "turn left." As I did I heard "take what would be your tithe and sow it to the one I show you." As I kept driving I ended up at a supercenter store, now my tithe was $40 at that time I earned by helping out a friend. As I parked I noticed a car to my right I saw headlights pull up. Not really paying it any mind I went through the store looking for the right person to bless. At first I did what most believers do in making the mistake of thinking we can see the hurt and need from the people to whom we are sent to minister. I was looking for someone broke-down, someone who looked as if they couldn't pay the tab on their grocery list. Well those things didn't happen and I walked out slightly disappointed thinking I must not have heard God correctly or I've disobeyed Him. Then I was approached by this young girl around 24yrs old and she says to me that her mom needed twenty dollars to get a bus ticket to Montgomery because her step-dad was beating on her mother. I then told her that I would be right back because I had to go to the ATM to get the cash. I noticed that she walked to the very car I saw pull up right as I was parking before I went into the store. I went to the ATM machine to get not $20, but $40 because that's what the Spirit told me to give, I took it to her and her mother and prayed that they'd be blessed. Even in this situation I learned that you can't judge a book by its cover and to obey God's word no matter what it looks like. We also see because I simply obeyed God that He worked through me to answer the prayers of the girl and her mother. God speaks to his servants in the earth realm (like me) and he allowed us to be at the same place at the same time so His power and glory and will be done.

Being Called Out By God

In 2010 God confirmed His promise to my prayers when He spoke to me through a prophet visiting the church I belonged to one night. The title of his Sermon was: "I can feel something Coming". In front of about 1,200 people while in the middle of his sermon he stops and looks me in my face while I was in worship; and say's "Do you hear me talking to you!?" He told me that "there was a demon assigned to me to destroy me and that he, the prophet, had just saved my Life!" Throughout his sermon he would confirm many things God had already spoke to me in my time in the car, and how some of the people there were part of my journey. Now, King David was never told that a demon was assigned to him, but Nathan the prophet in David's life, constantly confirm the things God was saying over the king's life. This particular night clearly explained to me that it was time out for playing around and get to doing God's work. It also confirmed the prayer I prayed when I was fourteen that it was now time to get to work.

Be aware of your Demons

I left the church that night pumped up with a zeal that would reach the clouds! Running to do the vision God had shown me time after time. Although I was on fire I missed one important word out of the prophet's sermon; and that was, "there was a demon assigned to me!" One of the biggest things that you need to know about the process is that there will always be a demon assigned to YOU. The bible puts it this way in Romans 7:21 –So I find this law at work: Although I want to do good, evil is right there with me (NIV). This law is also applied to our Lord and savior Jesus Christ when Jesus was baptized he was led into the wilderness for forty days and forty nights. We ALL have a demon assigned to us! This is important to know on your walk with Christ Jesus that the enemy is always seeking to destroy whom he may devourer. So it's important to keep on the whole armor of God spoken in scripture in Ephesians 6:10-18. My demon was my lust in women and although I was being very celibate in my new walk with Christ I was in search for a wife. That night the prophet spoke to me he made mention of me getting married by the time I was 33 years old, but just like I went into the supercenter looking for the right one to bless I went looking for the right woman. I had a casual friendship with a woman I met in the church and one Saturday went to a service together. As we walked into the building we saw a fellow church member standing at the door. Now I have no doubt that the fellow member was at the church the night the prophet spoke over my life because as we walked in the church they whisper in my ear, "hey that's your wife"!

If I knew then what I know now!

I took the advice of the whisperer to take the young woman in consideration to be my wife. Now demons work in groups – one was I couldn't seem to shake my lust of women although I was walking straight and narrow. Second were the lies they "whispered" in my ear which influenced me to believe with eyes and not my heart, although I knew what God had promised me! Needless to say I took the advice and started dating my once casual friend and having relations with her before marriage. This led me to asking for her hand in marriage and all the rest of the demons would then show up. There is a quote I once read in my pastors book that said "too much too fast too soon equals disaster". This quote does not always mean to be given things, like relationships, too fast too much for yourself you can disqualify yourself for what's next in your life. We ought to be thankful for a God who gives grace and his mercy toward us. Because God doesn't make mistakes people do and he's able to present a new opportunity after we've tried to take things too much and too fast. When I tried to get involved too soon with the woman that was suggested it caused lots of turmoil in my life. We had lots of differences the way we saw life and temperaments were not the same and scripture states; how can two walk together less they agree? Once I ended the relationship it caused plenty of people in the church to look at me with judgmental eyes. There is nothing worse than feeling alone in a place that was once so safe, it left me feeling betrayed and tainted by hurt. We parted ways but not without her mentioning it to the people in my life who've mentored me and trusted me with ministry. As painful as the situation was for me the church never pushed me out, I felt ashamed that my integrity was ruined. These mistakes were caused by my disobedience because God chastens those whom he loves and I was learning a great deal that I never wanted to feel this way again. I can remember coming to the end of myself and falling on my knees and asking God to fix it, however it needed to be fixed or whatever needed to be done to fix my life so I could live a life in Christ Jesus forever.

Before I made the first mistake in choosing the friend for a mate I had been celibate for a year. After I made the mistake of acting as if we were married I went celibate another year trusting God for the right mate; a wife who he would prepare for me. It was difficult trying to move on once everyone in the church caught drift to what I was doing wrong. But the one thing I know you can count on once you've made a mistake in God and that's his grace. I went back to work, continued serving in church and I served in church not worrying about the whispers and side looks anymore. I focused on what God wanted to do for me and to me, that mattered more than the opinion of what anyone could say or think of me. I wanted God, I wanted a Christ-like life, and the things of God matter more to me than the things of men and for that reason alone I will forever praise him. I am committed to love Jesus no matter what and as I stay committed to the process God will always reveal his favor toward me. A season arrived in my life where I met the love of my life. Now I knew that this situation could not end up like the last relationship I created on my own; I had to be sure that it was of God's doing and not my own. I had been serving under my mentor for at least a year and during the first season of meeting him I briefly met his daughter in the kitchen of their house while she was washing dishes.

How we met!

As I pulled up to the house that night I noticed this car with Mississippi plates parked almost in the middle of the road. So I went into the house and spoke to everyone and asked dad, my mentor; "whose car is that in the middle of the road with the Mississippi plates?" He replied Lucy's and I said to her sarcastically "that's not how we park here in Alabama, give me your key's so I can park it right!" That's how we met that day and that day moving forward we both served under my mentor and his wife Jackie Now we called them mom and dad, but we never addressed each other as brother and sister. When we meet I was still with the friend mentioned earlier and Lucy was dating the "wrong guy" in her hometown As time went on a year and a half later we both never saw each other in light of a relationship until we were really ready for a real relationship.

How we started!

After I started back working I would also maintain a social media ministry on the web trying to do my part in the kingdom. Well, as time went on I had not spoken to my mentor in about a year and I saw on the web that he was doing a baptism one weekend and I wanted to be there. So I asked him if he needed any help and he said sure if I can be there and if I knew of anyone else to bring them too. I got in touch with one of my friends from the church who was a barber because they wanted to give away free haircuts during the baptism. He and I went to the baptism to help and as I walked in there she was. Beautiful, tall, and sweet in her red top and long khaki skirt and her smile lit up the room. Very weird in a sense to me because I never saw her like this before and now I was here seeing her like I never had before. We first talked reminiscing over the times since we first met to then and exchanged numbers to speak later on. God has a way to keep you blind from the things right before your eyes until it's time for you to open them. It reminds me of the day Jesus spoke to Saul on the Damascus road after he said Saul, Saul why do you persecute me and after the conversation and instruction from Jesus he opened his eyes and could not see. Saul remained blind until the day his name was changed to Paul. Now I am no Paul, but I do believe God closed Lucy away from me until the right timing, after all God doesn't make mistakes people do!

Chapter 4 – Short Stories For You

These stories are told in short term scenarios of how God doesn't make mistakes people do. Stories of mistakes people have made and God used it for His Glory. These stories vary from the bible and real life situations. I Pray they open the eyes of your heart to see, just as he blessed me, he can and will bless you the same way.

ABRAHAM

Abraham is the father of many nations as we all know. Well before he obtained this promise Abraham made "plenty" of mistakes and was still chosen to be the father of many nations. One mistake was the day Abraham listens to his wife Sarah to go sleep with his maid servant to have a child with her because Sarah was thought to be barren. This mistake caused havoc in the household with Abraham, Sarah, and their maid servant whose name was Hagar. Now God didn't stop them before the mistakes because he gives us free will but God did look at the situation. After it was said to have Hagar and her son put out of the colony, God first told Abraham that his first born was still going to be a great nation! Later God tells Abraham that he will still bare a son in his old age. The day God tells him this Sarah hears it and makes the mistake of laughing at the thought of her and Abraham having a child in their old age. Then God hears the laugh and rebukes Sarah and tells Abraham that their child is to be named Isaac which means "He laughs." One thing we see here is that sometimes you just may have to live with the stain of your mistake for the rest of your life. Now of course Sarah will only see love when she looks at Isaac, but she will forever know how he got the name. Isaac, as we all know, went on to continue his lineages through the bloodline all the way to birth our Lord and Savior Jesus Christ!

MELLO

Now, Mello is not the father of many nations though he has plenty children. He was a man who once got into trouble with the law in his hometown and before the law caught him he ran away to another state. He ran and was gone for ten years trying to survive without a steady job and he survived with the mother of his two children. The main thing he thought he was surviving without was God. It's an amazing story to think that a man and his family evaded the law for ten whole years. One thing you won't find in this story is happiness. He told me that toward the end of him running that he got tired of not being able to use his real name. He came to the end of himself and then he told me about his prayer. His family had left him and when they left he went even farther away from where he was to another town off deep in the woods where no one would find him. He knew he couldn't run any longer on the path he'd created and now he was willing to face the mistakes that caused him to run in the first place. His story sounds a lot like the prodigal son when he ran and spent the inheritance his father gave him only to realize he'd made a mistake while sitting in a pigpen. The prayer he told me about came when he was standing outside on a rainy day. He said God if it is time to go home and turn myself in give me a sign. Soon after he prayed thunder hit very loud and it shocked him. He questioned if it was God so he prayed again, "God if it was you please show me another sign" and then thunder hit again "BOOM"! After the second thunder hit he said he wasn't going to ask again because the next time it might hit him. He called me and said he was ready to come home and I went to get him and took him to his hometown. He came on a day his father so happened to be in town. He had not talked with him since before he started running and ended up reunited with his family in the same day. He spent time with the family for two days and then the time came to turn himself in to the authorities. A day later he stood before the judge and the judge sentenced him to fifty hours of community service and dropped the other two charges he was facing. WOW. You mean that after running for ten years, having your name on the most wanted list and facing 2 years' minimum in prison all he got was community service? Yes. What a testimony because God forgave his sin and God didn't make the mistake he did.

JONAH

He ran as well towards another country out of his disobedience to do what God told him to do. God had sent Jonah to Nineveh, but he was trying to go to Tarshish. On his way he went through a near death experience inside the belly of a fish and it was there that he finds himself praying to God. Although he almost died after making the mistake of disobeying God, the Lord still favored him and his purpose to go and preach to the people of Nineveh. Looking at Jonah; he was a moody, disobedient, and stubborn man who pouted when things were not going his way, but he knew he feared and heard from God. God continued to do a work in Jonah, he also had compassion on the people of Nineveh because they fasted, prayed and asked God for forgiveness.

DANIEL

Daniel was a man falsely accused and sentenced to the lion's den. It all started when he was caught praying three times a day to God trusting in his faith in God and not man. Officers of the king saw Daniel and reprimanded him because there was a decree that banned anyone from praying to any god other than the king. Now the king loved Daniel but it troubled his heart when Daniel was brought before him but had no choice but the enforce his law. Daniel was then thrown into the lion's den for making the mistake of disobeying the law. Although he was accused and sentenced by law, God saw Daniel's charge as obedience to Him and not to man's law. God then shut the lion's mouths and no harm was brought to Daniel. Not only did God protect Daniel, but he was also promoted to a higher position, his prosecutors were devoured by the lions and the king's faith in God increased. God has a way of turning what man would call a mistake into a miracle. This was a man who just wanted to obey God at any cost even if it meant believing God unto death. He trusted that God was his help his provider and protection God was everything to Daniel.

MALIK

Now the short story that I am about to tell you is very dear to my heart. Malik is our youngest son. This story actually began long before Malik was born and starts when my wife was in her mid-twenties. She often used a phrase "I'm not going to have any children, I'm ok with my nieces and nephews"! She also has a god-daughter she claims as her own. She became more comfortable with speaking this over her life once her doctor began telling her she probably couldn't have kids. There was also another phrase she would use and that was "I don't have to be married". Well you know how that went because I've already addressed her as my wife several times.

After we got married I remember going to that same doctor. I went with her because we were praying on having a child. After reassuring us she couldn't get pregnant he sat us down and gave us the story about a guy on the roof of a house that was in a flood. The guy prayed for help and ended up having a conversation with God when he died because he didn't except the help God sent. In other words, he said that if we were going to have a child we needed help that would include hormone injections to help balance our chemistry. We heard his advice, but we decided to trust that God would bless us with a child. I later had a vision of a child playing in our living room and I knew it was God confirming what we're believing Him for. Later that same year my wife got pregnant and we got excited because we knew he'd answered our prayers. Shortly after there was a hard blow to the heart, we miscarried. Of course we were in a world of defeat thinking that the doctor was right and we might need help. That help was going to cost us $1200 dollars honestly our minds swayed a little but, we decided to trust that God would answer our prayers.

A year later we got pregnant again and shorty after there was another miscarriage. This second time around caused friction in our marriage and depression. Another doctor told us that we were not going to be able to make it happen. Well that's the big problem with a lot of believers we tend to try to help God! We say we completely trust Him and at the first sign of trouble we offer help to a God who needs no help at all. Yes, we were in pain but, we wouldn't give up on God. We went to a retreat that year and my spiritual dad told us to get up and dance to music that God was ministering to our seed. We danced and cried and left that retreat with joy still believing God.

That Christmas we had Kaleigh and Khalil with us for the holiday my children from previous relationships. While they were sleeping my wife took a pregnancy test and it came up positive! This time we knew God was answering or prayers. You see in hard times after you've been praying and waiting for your blessing you have to stick with trusting God! One reason you can bank on in waiting is that God is often not saying no but, not yet! Those doctors thought we were making a mistake in trusting God but, we knew that God would always have the last say so! My wife conceived and carried our son with no hormone help at all. We trusted that our Heavenly Father heard our prayers and nine months later we gave birth to a baby boy 8 lbs. and 22 1/2inches long. Our blessing, Malik!

Chapter 5 - Lessons Learned,
Earned, and Un-learned

I applied my heart to what I observed and learned a lesson from what I saw.

Proverbs 24:32 (NIV)

I've learned to trust God when I can't trace God! The first thing I would like to say is that God is real and just to look at the things I've expressed in this book is evidence that He is. I learned to listen to that still small voice that speaks to me from God and to trust God even when I can't trace Him. In my wilderness situation, there were times I thought that I was alone and what got me through it was learning the fact that I know, that I know, that I know I can trust God. Let's take a look back at the short stories to start. To start, we see that Abraham was a man who trusted God when God was not a popular topic in the land for the people. Yet, he still believed God and stayed close to God's direction his whole life even at 99 years of age believing that he would still have a child. This story also shows us that it's never too late for God to bless us in any shape form or fashion. It's simple to God since he created the world in seven days with just a spoken word. The blessings we look for seem huge but to Him its simpler than the stroke of a pen, He just speaks things into existence. We also see Mello the guy who ran for ten years thinking if he'd ever faced his mistakes he would be punished for them, but God! Now knowing that fear doesn't come from God, but from the enemy the devil. God used Mello's fear to allow him to run only to show him that God can turn any situation around just like that! It's never too late for Him to do anything for his own children. God can give the devil what he thinks is a head start only to let him come back to the realization that he will always lose because he is already defeated.

A great example of this is in the book of Job Chapter 1:6-12 when the angels and Satan stood before the Lord. God asked Satan where has he been and he replied that he was looking for whom he could devour. Then God pointed Satan into the direction of Job, a man who feared and trusted in Him. Then God said that everything he has is in your power Satan but don't lay a finger on Job. Satan went on to destroy everything Job had: his children, his land, and all to the point that had his wife wanted him to curse God and die. Then Satan and God had another conversation that leads God pointing Satan back into Job's direction. Evidently Satan didn't get the job done to make Job turn his back on God the first time even though he done all those things to Job. Later, after all Satan's failed attempts, we see Job restored and God gets the glory out of the situation. God allowed the hurt to come upon Job from the enemy only to show Satan that he cannot win in any test when it comes to God. Sometimes the test is not just to make you stronger, but also to show the enemy how mighty God's power is in his children. Believe me when I say God is bigger than anything you can go through and when I can't feel His presence or see what He's doing I know He always has my best interest at heart.

Quick note: If you can remember I mentioned a preacher earlier whose hands were drenched in oil. They were for healing we find this in scripture in the book of James 5:14 Is anyone sick among you? Let them call the elders of the church to pray over them and anoint them with oil in the name of the Lord. So now when you see this in church do not be alarmed it is the Word of God being performed for your good.

I've learned to choose Life in all situations!

This day I call the heavens and the earth as witnesses against you that I have set before you the (choice) between life and death, blessings and curses. "Now" choose life, so that you and your children may live and that you may love the LORD your God, "listen to his voice, and hold fast to him. For the LORD is your life, . . . and he swore to give to your fathers, Abraham, Isaac and Jacob.

Deuteronomy 30:19-20

The tongue has the power of life and death, and those who love it will eat its fruit.

Proverbs 18:21

These scriptures show us that God gives us the ability of free will. Yes, we have the ability to choose life and death in every situation. I met a man in 2015 at my job while writing this book and he gave me his testimony of when he heard God for the first time. He is originally from Africa and once roamed the streets of Greece as a teenager. One day he and a childhood friend of his were out adventuring the streets and saw this guy drop his wallet. He picked up the wallet looked inside of it and saw a large amount of money inside. His friend said to him to take the wallet and go because they had not eaten that day and didn't have money to buy anything. With the peer pressure of his friend saying let's get something to eat while he was hungry a still small voice said to him "it doesn't belong to you"! Still with his friend pressuring him to keep it he runs and gives the guy back his wallet telling him he dropped it along his path. The man took a look at the wallet thanked him, with no reward, and walked away. He was still hungry, his friend was angry and he questioned if he'd done the right thing or not. Later on that night they realized they had gotten too far from home and fell asleep on the ground. He felt a warm heat close to his face opened his eyes and noticed a stranger holding a cigarette to his face. Without any reason the strangers punched them and beat them and he and his friend thought they were going to die.

While he was getting beaten he searched for his friend with his eyes and saw that he was taken down the street. He told me he remembered praying that God would get them out of this situation and then he saw another person come up and stop the guys from beating them. The guy who walked up stopped the strangers and picked him up and asked if he was ok. Then he pulled out his wallet and gave him some money; he looked in amazement at the guy's face to find that it was the same guy who'd dropped his wallet earlier that day. He and his friend ate well that night. Although they were in pain they were happy they were alive and full of food. The choice he made to listen to the voice of doing the right thing paid the price of freedom out of a trap the enemy had set for them. He could have made the "mistake" to not listen to that voice, but God. No one knows what would have happened to them had not the guy shown up during the beating, but God. God set the option before him earlier that day to keep the wallet or give it back and he made the choice to trust the voice of the Holy Spirit and it paid the price of life! We have that same option set before us on a daily basis to choose between life and death good and bad to journey toward heaven or hell. This also is why I know that making the choice to accept Jesus as your Lord and personal savior is the best choice you can ever make in your life.

Lessons Earned!

Most of us learned the lesson of HOT as a child in the case of our parents telling us not to touch the stove or something hot. We really didn't understand it until we got burned! Then the child would touch the hot thing and scream "hot!" Well in the same notion of learning hot we learn a lot of what God is teaching us through our mistakes. In Philippians 4:11 says: *Not that I speak in respect of want: for I have learned; in whatsoever state I am, therewith to be content.* Before we accept Jesus as our Lord and savior we are often content in doing wrong and, because of that, we collect plenty of mistakes. I was one who was content in doing wrong before living a lifestyle of a Christian. I'd party, drink and enjoyed my folly as a sinner until I came to realize that I was hurting myself and the ones I loved. I allowed my children to see me with other women not understanding my stability as a father. Drinking was a regular habit of the weekend that left me broke and unable to pay my bills, I was always in a state of depression. It was then, at the end of all those things, when I came to the end of myself! I realized that my routine of doing wrong was killing me in debt, family, and in health. There would be times I would go to clubs with 700 dollars of my paycheck and wake up the next morning with 200 dollars wondering how I was going to make rent. There were friends and family members wondering if I was on drugs because I stayed broke all the time. Instead of quitting my habit I would get into the whirlwind of borrowing money from payday loans accumulating four loans at one time. Instead of paying my bills I was only paying the loans interest which left me broke again and I couldn't even think about putting anything in the church. I had to do something different. I remember getting on the floor of my apartment prostrate saying "Lord I surrender, I surrender" praying that there is nothing else I can do and it will only take you to get me out of my mess! It was only then that my life took a massive turnaround; I started looking for a church home and that day I heard the preacher say if you're not growing where you're going come visit us.

That same day I went and remember joining and understanding the word of God like never before. I learned the word from his teaching and also reading and learning for myself. I learned scriptures that I never thought I could remember like: 2 Tim. 2:15 Study to show thyself approved. And Romans 3:28 for we maintain that a person is justified by faith apart from the works of the law. That brings me to say I learned "hot" by experiencing that I was headed into an eternal heated situation, but by faith in Christ Jesus being redeemed from sin and heading toward salvation that it was only by His Grace that I was still alive. Grace allowed me to see that if I continue to live a life of folly I will only become a fool. My health, my finances and family needed to be built by God and His Grace allowed me to realize that. I didn't earn my lessons by doing the wrong things, but I learned my lesson by giving them to God through Christ. I learned by diligently seeking him through the word of God and serving Him in any way I thought I could. Putting God first in everything in my life allowed me to see my faults. I saw the hot situations I was creating in my life. It's amazing how you could be blinded by the enemy to self-satisfying the flesh that would lead you down a road of destruction. But by Grace in Jesus he justified me and set me on a path to help others see their wrongs and help them come out of their mess. The point came when I was fully committed to putting God first. I saw my finances get better as I trusted Him and paid my tithes. My health got better when I realized that if I wanted a long life to see my children and their children it would only be God's grace to get me there. As I cut out my mess God blessed my life and changed my situations. I realized that I am the lender and not the borrower. I am above and in control of how I handle what life brings by the power in Christ Jesus and he won't let me fail; he turns our mistakes into Miracles.

Unlearned

Being transformed by the renewing of the mind is unlearning a lot of the wrong habits we accumulate through life. Not just doing the right things but changing the way we live and think. One day after Jesus was crucified on the cross, Peter and some of the disciples with him went fishing and they noticed a man standing on the shore. The man on the shore first asked if they've caught any fish and they told him that they've been out on the water all night and haven't caught any fish. So the man on the shore told them to throw their net on the right side of the boat and they caught 153 fish. Then the bible says that in that moment they knew it was Jesus. One decision separated them from not catching fish to catching more than enough. The decision wasn't throwing the net on the right side of the boat, but it was taking time to listen to Jesus. Even when they couldn't recognize his face they still trusted his Word. You see even people who had been close to Jesus, right hand man close, made mistakes. We know Peter denied Jesus three times and afterwards he was so ashamed that he went back to doing what Jesus called him out of. We have to get to the mindset to think like Jesus, to give people grace in every situation and to think hope in hopeless situations. Let this mind be in you that was also in Christ Jesus. When we can do our best to think like Jesus, we can do our best to act like Jesus. I promise you we make fewer mistakes when we go with God.

My Prayer for you

Once you see that God doesn't make mistakes people do, we grow through what we go through and that makes us uniquely who we are. I was a mess in stress and I couldn't find my way out until I saw that Jesus was with me the whole time. It was His grace, His love for me that allowed Him to use what I had been through to help someone else get through their storms. Not only did I come out, I came out better than when I started once I learned to trust God when I couldn't trace God. Living in a car is never anything I would recommend, but it showed me that I can survive anything with Christ Jesus. Besides, God has already scripted our end so we can always trust Him through difficult times. My purpose in writing this book is to share my testimony, God gets the glory and prayerfully someone accepts Jesus as their Savior. So I pray:

Dear God,

As we pray to you we thank you for being our God for you alone are worthy to be praised. Not only are you worthy, we thank you for sending your only begotten son Jesus the Christ to come teach, show us the way, and die for our sins as a ransom for our salvation. Also, we thank you for sending your Holy Spirit to comfort us in times of need and to give us the power to withstand anything. So God, we thank you right now that those who read this book saw themselves in it. That they saw the situations in their lives changeable; changeable in a way that will shape them into a whole new being in Christ Jesus because if Jesus could bring me out of my mess with the mistakes I've made in life, you can do the same for them. We know that calling our downfalls mistakes does not mean we didn't sin, but we recognize that we all have sinned and fallen short of the glory of God, but to know that the promises of God are yes and amen, meaning that what you've spoken over our lives even before we were placed in our mother's womb. The promise would not go undone and that everything you spoke will be established until the day of Christ Jesus. That you reward those who diligently seek you redeeming them by grace giving them double for the trouble making their latter years greater than their past. Also that we will all learn to see with our ears and listen with our eyes to remain teachable and sensitive to your Holy Spirit and your ways; that we won't miss your blessings because of our own mistakes. I pray that you will teach us how to receive each blessing and teach us how redistribute them in Jesus the Christ name I pray.

Amen

coming soon. . .

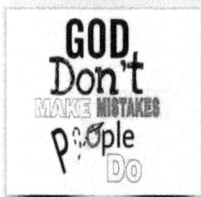

visit us @
www.Goddontmmpeopledo.com

ALSO FOLLOW US ON:

@GDMMPDO

@GodDontMMPPLDo